"Iran on Notice: The Future of U. S. Policy on Iran"

United States House of Representatives

Committee on Foreign Affairs

February 16, 2017

ISBN   1544030010

ISBN-10   978-1544030012

Table of Contents

"Iran on Notice: The Future of U. S. Policy on Iran"

Prepared testimony of Scott Modell
Managing Director, The Rapidan Group

"Iran on Notice: The Future of U.S. Policy Toward Iran"

Prepared testimony of Scott Modell
Managing Director, The Rapidan Group
Before the House of Representatives Committee on Foreign Affairs

February 16, 2017

Chairmen Royce, Ranking Member Engel, Members of the Committee, thank you for the opportunity to testify today. The election of Donald Trump and the apparent willingness of his national security team to sharpen U.S. policy toward Iran allow us to consider hard-hitting policy recommendations that were anathema to President Obama's softer, more conciliatory approach during the past eight years. A tougher approach should target the decayed base of popular support for the regime, ratchet up international law enforcement efforts, take advantage of increasingly intractable problems within the regime itself, and the lay the foundation for a multi-year effort to change the behavior of the regime. Despite all of its shortcomings and failings, however, the Islamic Republic is not on the verge of collapse. In the graphic below, the conditions for a "Persian spring" or even major reform are not present:

The Evolution of Change Indicators in Iran				
Leading indicators of change	Dec 1979	May 1996	May 2009	Feb 2017
Regime no longer functional	Yes	Somewhat	Somewhat	Somewhat
Economic downturn	Yes	Yes	Yes	Yes
Security services undermined	No	No	No	No
Political elite infighting	Yes	Somewhat	Somewhat	Somewhat
Elite support to opposition	No	No	Somewhat	No
Widespread popular dissatisfaction	Yes	Yes	Yes	Yes
Willingness to protest	Yes	No	Yes	No
Organized resistance	Yes	No	Yes	No
Charismatic leader	Yes	No	Somewhat	No
Tools to effectively communicate	Yes	No	Somewhat	Yes
	Why Khomeini won then…			…and why change is unlikely

Instead, the recommendations below argue for increasing military and non-military pressure to moderate regime behavior over time. If implemented, they would add some heft to the decision by former National Security Advisor Flynn to put Iran on notice, strengthen our own national security apparatus in the process, and send a clear signal that we intend to hold Iran accountable for its illicit and destabilizing activities.

Recommendation #1: Overhaul Voice of America (VOA) and Radio Free Europe (RFE)'s "Radio Farda." Ratings have hit rock bottom due to watered down programming, low morale, and the corrosive and undermining presence of regime apologists who often do a better job justifying Iran's nuclear program than the regime itself. There is no excuse for this, especially given the low credibility of government controlled media. A revitalized Persian media offensive has a target rich, anti-regime Iranian audience: 50 million regular viewers of satellite TV, 44 million internet users, 20 million users of social networks and "secure" messaging apps, and 18 million smart phones (all mostly used by youth). Suggested reforms include the following:

- In addition to programmatic changes, VOA and RFE should have a strict policy of employee screening. Existing background checks are inadequate, even on Iranians coming directly from IRIB and other Iranian govt. ministries. It would be fairly easy for a sophisticated intelligence service such as Iran's MOIS to infiltrate VOA and RFE and take the edge off of anti-regime programming.
- Deeply integrate VOA and RFE with U.S. Iran policy. VOA and RFE should go beyond reporting the news. They should also be platforms for explaining U.S. policy, exploiting divisions and conflicts within the regime, bolstering reformists and calling for free and fair elections, weakening international support for Iran, and highlighting Iran's links to regional destabilization. VOA should create a "Window to Washington" program on U.S. policy.
- Compound the impact of existing fissures in Iran: While the Green Movement is either dead or on life support, protests do occur on a very regular basis across the country. Persian media outlets should be shining a light on protestors, from angry factory workers and ethnic groups to women's rights activists and impoverished teachers. Even though these protests tend to be local and short-lived, we should help these "unconnected clusters of dissent" coalesce and lead to stronger anti-regime behavior. Congress should mandate regular reports from the Administration on the foreign policy value of U.S.-sponsored Persian media programs.
- Countering regime efforts to block transmissions: Congress should ensure VOA, RFE, and others have the capability to broadcast even when the regime blocks incoming transmission. This could include the use of wireless signals (WIMAX) into areas such as Iranian Kurdistan where the govt. regularly blocks foreign media signals. Our allies in the region have potential roles to play in this regard.
- Include programs that expose the interconnectivity between the IRGC's existing economic empire and corruption. Investigations into the illicit networks of Reza Zarrab and Babak Zanjani alone could fill dozens of hours of air time. VOA and RFE should amplify their reporting on corruption by building on the work of popular shows such as the Last Page ("Safhe-ye Akhar").

Recommendation #2: Use the reforms to Persian media mentioned above to spearhead an information warfare campaign against Iran. In addition to highlighting ties to terrorism and corruption, U.S.-led efforts should focus on harnessing the untapped anger, resentment, and willingness to speak out against the regime.

- Women: The women's movement in Iran is more about recapturing the rights women used to have. Nobel Laureate, Shirin Ebadi, was a judge before the 1979 Islamic Revolution. Today, women are prohibited by law from becoming judges. No social group has lost as much as women in the Islamic Republic, and no issue packs more hidden energy in Iran than women's rights and gender equality.

- Teachers and other low wage earners: The regime's inability to counter growing inequality and poverty is a growing problem. Efforts have failed and the regime has no plan for lifting the growing mass of low wage earners above the poverty line. The results is evident in some sort of strike or demonstration almost every day in Iran.
- Ethnic Groups: Several are so disenfranchised in the Islamic Republic that they are not allowed to name their children in their native languages. The regime has prevented the construction of a Sunni mosque in Tehran, despite the more than one million Sunni residents. The plight of Azeri, Baluch, and other ethnic minorities are important axes of Iran's dysfunctional civil society.
- Social Crises: The regime's malfeasance has created a number of crises in areas from health to welfare, each of which has spurred the creation of small but organized movements. Record levels of air pollution in Tehran and other major cities, harmful radiation due to government interference with satellite TV signals, high youth unemployment, drug addiction, and rampant prostitution.

Recommendation #3: Declassify intelligence that shows the links between Iran, al-Qa'ida, the Taliban, and violent Sunni and Shia terrorist groups. Iran has successfully hijacked the "global war on terror" narrative that used to be led by the United States. Today, it effectively markets itself as the leading state sponsor of counter-terrorism. This exposure should extend to the drug trade.

- Links between al-Qa'ida and Iran's security services exist and should be exploited as part of the media campaign mentioned above. It would undermine Iran's self-proclaimed status on the front lines of the war against radical Islam, while further eroding domestic support for the last generation's revolutionary zeal.
- This should go hand in hand with releases of similar information on GCC support to Sunni extremists. US credibility will benefit most if we air the dirty laundry of all sides. Deputy Crown Prince Mohamed bin Salman (MbS) and his generation could become effective partners in this regard as they attempt to rebrand the Kingdom.
- Iran's hand in drug trafficking, both inside Iran and across the region, should be further explored and exploited. Several international narcotics trafficking investigations have pointed to IRGC involvement, either in distribution inside Iran or in transit on the way to Turkey and ultimately Europe and the United States.

Recommendation #4: Expand and facilitate the PL-110 program. There are few incentives for well-placed individuals inside the Iranian government to risk their lives to cooperate with the U.S. government. Congress should broaden PL-110 authorities to increase the number of aliens U.S. government agencies can bring into the United States every year. The process is lengthy, cumbersome, and overly restrictive.

- D/CIA has the right to give away 100 green cards every year to individuals who provide extraordinary assistance to U.S. intelligence collection and covert action efforts. This number should increase dramatically in order to increase the number of potential defectors and to stimulate the "brain drain" of Iranian scientists and senior technocrats from government agencies overseeing Iran's most sensitive nuclear and conventional military sites, ongoing R&D, strategic policy, and illicit procurement. We should encourage our European counterparts to do the same.

- PL-110 should not be limited to intelligence activities. We should also reward those who enable international law enforcement efforts. Investigations and operations that lead to the identification, arrest, and even extradition of individuals involved in activities that violate the JCPOA, support terrorist proxies, etc.
- An expansion of PL-110 could go hand in hand with a reinvigorated Treasury attache cadre in areas around the world that are vulnerable to transnational organized crime. Sanctions, designations, and other Treasury actions from Washington can only go so far. Our overseas national security and diplomatic corps has a very limited understanding of threat finance, stunting the development of working-level law enforcement relationships.

Recommendation #5: Expose the scope of Iranian corruption and human rights abuse by adding Iranian individuals to the Magnitsky List, or by creating one specific to Iran. Most Iranians are well aware of the staggering depth of corruption in Iran today, particularly among the IRGC and conservative power elite. Even President Rouhani routinely regards corruption as one of the largest failures of the Islamic Revolution.

- Congress should pass legislation calling on the Administration to produce quarterly reports on Iranian government corruption and violations of human rights. The unclassified report would further delegitimize Iran's ruling class, enable democratic and reform-minded elites in Iran, serve as fodder for English and Persian media, and underscore U.S. support to the silent majority of Iranians who are increasingly disconnected to the Islamic Revolution.
- Congress should also provide funding for U.S. government website upgrades. Efforts to denigrate the regime would be well served if our own law enforcement websites had the capacity to serve as secure transceivers of valuable information. Doing so would occasionally uncover compromising information that could be exploited in social media, used in law enforcement investigations, or disseminated to companies that are either active in Iran or considering the possibility.
- Crime matrix: Treasury or State should have a website with a matrix that lists individuals and entities in Iran followed by their involvement in or links to corruption, human rights violations, terrorism, money laundering, drug trafficking, nuclear proliferation, etc. The worst offenders of the regime should be highlighted up front, from the Supreme Leader himself and his closest financial managers such as Vahid Haqqanian and Mohammad Mokhber to the head of finance for the Astan-e Qods Foundation, Sayyed Morteza Bakhtiari.

Recommendation #6: Bolster Najaf, Iran's main rival in the competition for leadership over the worldwide Shia community. Najaf in Iraq and Qom in Iran have long struggled to be the primary "source of emulation" for Shiites around the world. Iran's model is a theocracy that puts the clergy in positions of political power, whereas Iraq's leading authority Grand Ayatollah Sistani sticks to a more orthodox interpretation of Shia Islam that encourages the clergy to steer clear of politics.

- We should encourage Arab allies to openly support Najaf's more tolerant "quietist" traditions, particularly important in the run-up to a possible succession of Supreme Leader Khamenei in Iran and the passing on of the 86 year-old Sistani.
- This should involve the promotion of the most prominent and revered figures in Iran such as Ayatollah Shirazi and others (who are against Khamenei) and in Iraq who support more

tolerant and less militant and politicized forms of Shia Islam. Iran is aggressively involved in a soft war to undermine support for Sistani and other Grand Ayatollahs likely to replace him.

Recommendation #7: Change the rules of engagement. IRGC fast boats swarming U.S. vessels is one dimension of a sustained pattern of provocation in the Gulf. There were at least 35 such "close encounters" in 2016 alone, a constant reminder of Iran's threat to commercial traffic carrying 17 million barrels per day of oil and gas through the Strait of Hormuz.

- The U.S. should deal militarily with IRGC threats and harassment in the Gulf. Tough rhetoric and firing warning shots are not enough to deter Iranian aggression. New rules of engagement should be made clear to Iran in keeping with General Flynn's marker to put Iran on notice.
- U.S. should provide missile defense, security guarantees, and overt training and support to Bahrain and our GCC allies to deter and defend against the full spectrum of asymmetric threats posed by Iran.
- The U.S. should also encourage Saudi Arabia and its GCC partners to continue their regional strategy of pushing back against Iranian aggression across the region. As Riyadh in particular has learned in Syria and Yemen, there is a steep learning curve that will last for several years. On the other hand, Iran has been active in cyber war, proxy war, conventional war, and various forms of covert action for decades. If we ever hope to downsize our role, the GCC countries must do more to balance security in the region.

These are just a few recommendations for a new U.S. policy on Iran that focuses more intently on Iran's malign, destabilizing behavior across the region. I appreciate the opportunity to present them before the Committee.

"Iran on Notice: The Future of U. S. Policy on Iran"

Katherine Bauer
Blumenstein-Katz Family Fellow
Washington Institute for Near East Policy

Iran on Notice

Katherine Bauer
Blumenstein-Katz Family Fellow,
The Washington Institute for Near East Policy

Testimony submitted to the House Committee on Foreign Affairs
February 16, 2017

Chairman Royce, Ranking Member Engel, and members of the committee, thank you for the opportunity to appear before you to discuss the future of U.S. policy toward Iran. My testimony will focus on the role of sanctions in restraining Iran's malign influence in the region and disrupting its global-terrorism, money-laundering and procurement networks. Much of the following comes from analysis done in conjunction with my colleagues Patrick Clawson and Matthew Levitt at the Washington Institute for Near East Policy as part of a new study released earlier this week.[1]

INTRODUCTION

Following implementation of the Iran nuclear deal in January 2016, and suspension of nuclear-related sanctions, the pace of new Iran-related designations under remaining authorities slowed. Despite assurances that that United States would "vigorously press sanctions against Iranian activities outside of the Joint Comprehensive Plan of Action," [2] the Obama administration did so only sporadically. Thus, in many ways, Washington ceded the narrative to Tehran, which successfully convinced many in the private and public sectors that in the wake of implementation of the nuclear agreement, they operate in a "post-sanctions environment."

However, sanctions remain a viable and powerful tool for Congress and the new administration to confront Iran over human rights abuses, terror support, and ballistic missile tests. In our study, we suggest that the new administration adopt a multipronged approach to reinforcing the role of sanctions in restraining Iranian aggression in the region and other malign activities. This approach involves taking back the narrative about the deal by emphasizing the sanctions that remain; fully implementing those sanctions; imposing additional sanctions for nonnuclear transgressions; and applying proportional sanctions when Iran fails to comply with part of the nuclear deal.

Enhanced sanctions will work best if they are accompanied by diplomatic, military, and intelligence measures in a coordinated campaign against Iran's destabilizing activities. Likewise, sanctions are most effective when they are adopted by an international coalition. Foreign partners have long been skeptical of U.S. unilateral sanctions when they are viewed as being capricious. Focusing on Iranian conduct that violates international norms will thus be most likely to draw multilateral support. Relatedly, demonstrating international resolve on nonnuclear issues is more apt to garner Iranian respect for the constraints of the deal itself.

EMPHASIZE REMAINING SANCTIONS

The first component of this multipronged strategy is to change the narrative holding that sanctions are going away: this is not a post-sanctions environment, and Iran's ongoing illicit conduct is the reason for continued sanctions. Indeed, Iran made no commitment to cease nonnuclear malign activity and has not, in fact, halted it. In the words of Abbas Araqchi, Iran's deputy foreign minister and one of Iran's chief negotiators of the deal, "During the nuclear negotiations, we clearly said that questions of security, defense, ballistic missile and our regional policies were not negotiable and not linked to the nuclear talks."[3] In fact, according to the top U.S. military commander in the Middle East, Army Gen. Joseph Votel, Iran has been more aggressive regionally since implementation of the nuclear agreement.[4] Yet Iran is in complete control on this front: it can alter its behavior and cease engaging in illicit conduct, in which case sanctions will be removed. For the United States, rather than talking about reimposing suspended sanctions, which would receive strong pushback from U.S. allies, the narrative should be about exposing and disrupting persons and entities on still-sanctionable grounds.

Part of this new narrative involves repeating the statement that Iran remains subject to international norms. The idea is simple: "Iran gets no special pass." The nuclear accord does not prevent the imposition of nonnuclear sanctions or the use of other tools to contest such illicit conduct, just as arms treaties with the former Soviet Union did not spare it from other sanctions. Such an effort will be aimed, as noted, at changing the perception that sanctions are going away and the related Iranian narrative that any remaining restrictions signal bad faith by the United States.

Public statements should focus on the behavior that elicits sanctions, not the chilling impact they could have on investment in Iran or the uncertainty new sanctions would introduce. That said, the Trump administration should counter claims that the sanctions relief was "front-loaded" and make clear that a snapback of sanctions would have profound consequences for Iran. In doing so, Washington should emphasize that Iran still has much to lose—the bulk of Iran's no-longer-restricted assets remain offshore—and that renewed financial and commercial relationships remain tenuous. Statements should make a strong, direct case that Iran is violating international norms when it engages in deceptive behavior to deliver support to terrorist organizations; clandestine procurement for its missile program; use of information technology to suppress human rights; or violations of UN Security Council arms embargoes. The new U.S. administration should also make plain that the United States will expose and disrupt Iran's use of proxies to create plausible deniability and threaten asymmetric retaliation. The credibility of financial sanctions, and the ability to leverage them to build a multinational coalition, depends on responding directly to Iranian behavior and not casting sanctions-related actions as a tool of economic warfare.

Since the aim is to rally international support by showing that Iran rather than the United States is breaking the rules, sanctions enforcement should not be explained as a tactic to toughen the nuclear deal. Indeed, implying that the sanctions are meant to create uncertainty in the marketplace—to prevent Iran from benefiting from its yield from the nuclear deal—reinforces Iran's narrative that the United

States isn't living up to its commitments under the Joint Comprehensive Plan of Action (JCPOA), as the deal is known. Likewise, revising or rescinding technical guidance on sanctions relief risks delegitimizing the Office of Foreign Assets Control (OFAC) in its role as technical implementer of sanctions policy. After all, the guidance is a reflection of underlying statute and regulation and does not alter legal realities. Furthermore, many of the regulatory realities reflect positions taken across U.S. sanctions programs and are not specific to the Iran program. Across-the-board changes may have unintended consequences on other sanctions programs, whereas changing the rules only for Iran would complicate implementation.

Private-sector engagement on the risks of doing business with Iran opened up political space for European and Asian states to join in U.S.-led efforts to impose nuclear-related sanctions on the Islamic Republic. Given this history, the U.S. government should resume engagements with private- and public-sector actors around the world to highlight evidence that Iran continues to pose a threat to the global financial system. Rather than reassuring banks that doing business with Iran can help enshrine the nuclear deal, U.S. government officials at every level should emphasize that Iran bears the onus of demonstrating its adherence to the same requirements imposed on every other country by reining in illicit financial activity and conforming with international norms for its financial system. U.S. officials should also highlight the continued UN Security Council restrictions that Iran violates, including the embargo on Iranian arms exports extended under Security Council Resolution 2231 and the UN embargo on arming Hezbollah in Syria and the Houthis in Yemen. Recall that a number of Iranian individuals and entities sanctioned under earlier Security Council resolutions for their role in WMD procurement and weapons exports remain on the UN list. Also to be emphasized is that regional bodies concur with the United States that Hezbollah is a terrorist group—both the European Union and the Gulf Cooperation Council have designated Hezbollah in part or in full—and that Iranian human rights abusers are sanctionable not just by the United States but also by the EU. This will drive home the point that it is not only the United States that takes issue with Iran's illicit conduct and continues to sanction Iran.

Furthermore, U.S. officials should emphasize that when foreign firms face problems in doing business with Iran, deceptive practices by Iranian companies are to blame. The U.S. mantra should be that the more Iran complies with international norms, the easier will be its integration into the world economy. Whenever Iranian officials complain about hindered access to the international financial system, Washington should quickly respond that Tehran must first comply with the multinational Financial Action Task Force (FATF) standards on combating money laundering and terrorist financing.[5] Indeed, U.S. officials should point out that Iran must act quickly not only to meet FATF standards but also to adopt Basel III requirements established over the past five years, including on transparency in financial accounts. Further, if Iran expects to have normal transactions with foreign banks, it needs to allow for information sharing on tax compliance in line with U.S. Foreign Account Tax Compliance Act (FATCA) requirements and now the OECD-sponsored Common Reporting Standard System adopted by more than a hundred countries.[6] Whenever Iranian officials cite third-country concerns about U.S. penalties, Washington should respond that transparency from Iranian firms about their ownership would permit foreign businesses to easily comply with U.S. rules to avoid businesses affiliated with Iran's Islamic Revolutionary Guard Corps (IRGC).

Rather than talking about the sanctions that have been lifted, U.S. officials should emphasize the sanctions that remain. In citing the JCPOA chapter and verse, Washington can point to text that underscores the risks of Iranian misbehavior: the retention of sanctions authorities (sanctions are waived or suspended, not terminated) and potential for snapback; the limited list of sanctions removed, clearly indicating many remaining nonnuclear sanctions;[7] and footnotes that allow for abrogation of OFAC licenses should Iran misuse licensed aircraft.[8] Washington should then articulate that the flip side of its pledge not to introduce new nuclear sanctions is its reserved right to impose new sanctions for nonnuclear reasons. Such an approach lines up with the guiding principle suggested thus far: that the U.S. narrative should eschew a focus on sanctions going away while making clear that new sanctions do not represent a violation.

FULLY IMPLEMENT EXISTING SANCTIONS

The second element of the multipronged strategy is to intensify implementation of existing sanctions, since on a number of fronts, the Obama administration had been soft-pedaling the implementation of the existing sanctions designations.

Terrorism

More-vigorous action is needed against several Iran-sponsored entities subject to sanctions for involvement in terrorism.

First is the Qods Force (QF), the branch of the IRGC responsible for external operations and support to terrorist proxies. The QF has been Iran's primary means of providing training materials and financial support to proxies worldwide, including in the Middle East (Lebanon, Syria, Iraq, Yemen) but also beyond (e.g., Nigeria, Kenya, Latin America). New designations under existing counterterrorism executive authorities could target QF personnel and support networks, such as those in Lebanon, Syria and Yemen, as well as outside the region, such as in sub-Saharan Africa and Latin America. For example, Kenyan officials arrested two Iranians in late November 2016 outside the Israeli embassy in Nairobi, where they reportedly had been casing the facility. The two Iranians, in a vehicle with diplomatic plates, had just visited a prison where two other Iranians were being held on terrorism-related charges. According to Kenyan officials, the two jailed Iranians belong to the Qods Force, and were convicted on charges of plotting attacks against Western interests in Kenya in 2013.[9] Diplomatic engagements should also include efforts to enforce UN travel bans on QF-affiliated individuals, including its commander, Qasem Soleimani.[10]

Second is Mahan Air, which was designated in 2011 for providing support to the QF. Targeting such QF-related sanctions evaders—agents and financial fronts—would expose and disrupt networks that facilitate the QF's provision of assistance to Iranian proxies. Mahan Air continues to fly routinely to Syria,[11] possibly ferrying fighters and weapons. The airline also briefly made passenger flights from Tehran to Sana in the spring of 2015, not long after Houthi rebels took control of the Yemeni capital. These continued until the Saudi-led coalition bombed the tarmac to prevent a Mahan plane from landing.[12, 13] Despite remaining on U.S. sanctions lists, Mahan Air has opened new routes to Moscow, Kiev, Copenhagen, and Paris since January 2016.[14] The airline now reportedly flies to forty-three cities in twenty-nine countries, excluding Iran.[15]

The United States has taken only limited actions to highlight the risks of doing business with Mahan Air. In 2012, the U.S. Department of the Treasury attached sanctions to 117 aircraft belonging to Iran Air, Mahan Air, and Yas Air, alleging that Tehran was sending both Iran Air and Mahan Air flights to Damascus to deliver military and crowd-control equipment to the Assad regime.[16] Although the Iran

Air planes were removed from sanctions lists as part of the JCPOA, more than forty Mahan Air and Yas Air planes remain subject to U.S. sanctions, and as a result, foreign banks that deal with them risk losing access to the U.S. financial system. This risk applies not just to the aircraft but also to any dealings with the airline as a whole. In May 2015, the United States designated Iraq-based Al-Naser Airlines,[17] from which Mahan obtained nine aircraft, and in March 2016 designated Britain- and UAE-based front companies acting on Mahan's behalf.[18] In using sanctions authorities to expose Mahan's illicit activities and agents operating worldwide, the United States would support diplomatic efforts to encourage European, Asian, and Middle East states to ban Mahan flights, as Saudi Arabia did in April 2016,[19] as well as put pressure on commercial actors to curtail relationships with Mahan, considering the additional sanctions risks. For example, such efforts could entail public exposure through designation of intermediaries that provide Mahan ticketing and other financial services in Europe and Asia, where banks would be unlikely to work directly with Mahan given the risk of losing access to the U.S. financial system.

Third on the list of entities against which additional enforcement is needed is Hezbollah. The Hezbollah International Financing Prevention Act (HIFPA), which came into effect in March 2016, extends to Hezbollah secondary sanctions like those employed against Iran. Prior to HIFPA, a series of U.S. actions had already constrained Hezbollah's financial operations, and the new law has intensified the pressure. The Treasury Department assessed in July 2016 that Hezbollah is in "its worst financial shape in decades."[20] For his part, in a televised address the previous month, Hezbollah secretary-general Hassan Nasrallah had denied the impact of outside pressure on the organization's commercial and criminal ties, insisting that Hezbollah was funded solely by Iran. This was despite the bombing of a Lebanese bank earlier that month, widely believed to have been carried out by Hezbollah in response to the closure of reportedly hundreds of Hezbollah-related accounts by Lebanese banks, some of them arguably acting beyond the scope of the new U.S. law. While Lebanese regulatory authorities intervened to prevent so-called overcompliance with the U.S. law by local banks and forestall further confrontation with Hezbollah, additional U.S. designations of Hezbollah businessmen and businesses would give Lebanese banks cover to protect the Lebanese financial system from further abuse. Likewise, applying secondary sanctions under HIFPA to a financial institution banking Hezbollah or its associates outside the Middle East, such as in Africa or Latin America, would emphasize HIFPA's global reach and minimize the impact on Lebanon's financial sector.

Furthermore, investigations by U.S. and European law enforcement led to the revelation that Hezbollah's terrorist wing, the External Security Organization (aka the Islamic Jihad Organization), runs a dedicated entity specializing in worldwide drug trafficking and money laundering. This finding was made public in early 2016 by a joint operation that included the Drug Enforcement Administration (DEA), Customs and Border Protection, the Treasury Department, Europol, Eurojust, and authorities in France, Germany, Italy, and Belgium. The investigation spanned seven countries and led to the arrest of several members of Hezbollah's so-called Business Affairs Component (BAC) on charges of drug trafficking, money laundering, and procuring weapons for use in Syria.[21]

As a result of this transnational investigation, authorities arrested "top leaders" of the BAC's "European cell." These included Mohamad Noureddine, "a Lebanese money launderer who has worked directly with Hezbollah's financial apparatus to transfer Hezbollah funds" through his companies while maintaining "direct ties to Hezbollah commercial and terrorist elements in both Lebanon and Iraq." In January 2016, the Treasury Department had designated Noureddine and his partner, Hamdi Zaher El Dine, as Hezbollah terrorist operatives, noting that the group needs individuals like these "to launder criminal proceeds for use in terrorism and political destabilization."

The outing of the BAC resulted from a series of DEA cases run under the rubric of "Project Cassandra," which targeted "a global Hezbollah network responsible for the movement of large quantities of cocaine in the United States and Europe." But there are many other recent cases in which transnational organized criminal activities are carried out by people with formal, even senior ties to the group.

Consider the two operatives arrested in October 2015 for conspiring to launder narcotics proceeds and international arms trafficking on behalf of Hezbollah. Iman Kobeissi, arrested in Atlanta, had offered to launder drug money for an undercover agent and informed him that her associates in Hezbollah were seeking to purchase cocaine, weapons, and ammunition. Joseph Asmar, arrested in Paris the same day in a coordinated operation, also discussed potential narcotics transactions with an undercover agent, offering to use his connections with Hezbollah to provide security for drug shipments. In total, the suspects mentioned criminal contacts in at least ten countries around the world, highlighting the transnational nature of this Hezbollah-run operation.

Indeed, over the past eighteen months, the group's criminal facilitators have been arrested around the world, from Lithuania to Colombia and many points in between. Others have been designated by the Treasury Department, including Kassem Hejeij, a businessman with direct ties to Hezbollah; Husayn Ali Faour, a member of the Islamic Jihad Organization; and Abd Al Nur Shalan, a key Hezbollah weapons procurer who has close ties with the group's leadership. In the words of a senior Treasury official, "Hezbollah is using so-called legitimate businesses to fund, equip, and organize [its] subversive activities."

Under the Obama administration, however, these investigations were tamped down for fear of rocking the boat with Iran and jeopardizing the nuclear deal. Now, the Trump administration should aggressively target Hezbollah's financial, logistical, and procurement networks, including resurrecting the DEA's now-defunct Project Cassandra. The new administration should also pursue Hezbollah's BAC operatives with designations and arrests, as well as seek extradition of arrested Hezbollah facilitators in France, Colombia, Lithuania, and elsewhere, and thereafter indict them in U.S. courts.

Ballistic Missile Development and Conventional Arms Exports

Extension of ballistic missile and conventional arms restrictions on Iran for eight and five years, respectively, falls under UN Security Council Resolution 2231. Although UNSCR 2231 endorsed the JCPOA, Iran has said that it is bound only by the JCPOA and not the UN missile or arms restrictions, which it has long maintained are illegal. Since the JCPOA's implementation in January 2016, Iran has tested missiles on at least three separate occasions, most recently on January 29, 2017.[22] While UNSCR 2231 calls on Iran only to refrain from ballistic missile development—technically falling short of a ban—the resolution maintains sanctions, for the duration of the restrictions, on a number of Iranian individuals and entities involved in the country's ballistic missile program and arms exports. It also allows for new sanctions against those who act on behalf of those who remain on the list.

In addition to the remaining UN restrictions, U.S. sanctions continue to apply to a number of Iranian individuals and entities under Executive Order 13382, which applies financial sanctions to those involved in proliferation activities and their support networks.[23] Such nonproliferation sanctions can have a profound disruptive impact, since illicit procurement is often done under the guise of legitimate purchases of dual-use goods. These restrictions, however, have little meaning unless new entities are continuously added to the list of designated companies; otherwise, Iran will just create new shell fronts through which to evade the restrictions. The February 3, 2017, designation of several networks and supporters of Iran's ballistic missile procurement were the first such actions since the January 2016 designation of Mabrooka Trading for its role in missile-related procurement networks. In addition to targeting previously unknown or nonpublic fronts, robust implementation of nonproliferation sanctions ought to include continuing to identify affiliates of Iran's missile development complex, subagencies and commercial actors affiliated with the Ministry of Defense and Armed Forces Logistics (MODAFL), the Defense Industries Organization, the Aerospace Industries Organization, which has done much of their missile work, and other key missile entities, including Shahid Hemmat Industrial Group and Shahid Bakeri Industrial Group, along with additional Iranian officials cooperating with North Korea on missile development. The March 2016 sanctions that targeted subsidiaries of Shahid Hemmat Industrial and the IRGC Al-Ghadir Missile Command provide an example.[24]

Under the arms embargo of Security Council resolution 1747, adopted in March 2007, a number of Iranian individuals and entities were subjected to UN asset freezes and travel bans. These listings are maintained under the UNSCR 2231 regime. Notably, in 2012, Ali Akbar Tabatabaei, the commander of the IRGC-QF Africa Corps, was designated for overseeing weapons transfers in Africa, including a shipment intended for the Gambia by another sanctioned QF official, Hosein Aghajani.[25] The United States and UN also designated the earlier-mentioned Iranian cargo carrier Yas Air the same year for working with Hezbollah and Syrian officials to transfer weapons to Syria and the Tehran-based Behineh Trading Company for facilitating the entry of weapons and QF personnel into Nigeria.[26] In continuously updating these lists as new information becomes available, the United States must especially monitor Iranian arms transfers to Hezbollah in Syria and Houthi rebels in Yemen, and press for UN action in cases where sufficient evidence can be made public.

Human Rights Abuses

Beginning in 2010 and lasting through 2014, the United States levied a number of sanctions against Iranian commercial and governmental entities and officials for committing "serious human rights abuses" linked to the crackdown following the Iranian election in 2009. Among those sanctioned was the IRGC for the mistreatment of political detainees held in a ward of Tehran's Evin Prison, which operates under the Guards' control.[27] The sanctions also extended to the Basij and Iran's Law Enforcement Force, as well as to a number of senior security officials and government-related technology and telecommunications entities. However, no new human-rights-related designations have been made since implementation of the JCPOA.

Likewise, the EU has adopted a number of restrictive measures, including asset freezes and visa bans on individuals and entities responsible for committing human rights violations, as well as export bans on equipment that can be used for internal repression and monitoring telecommunications. Notably, the EU recently extended until April 2017 travel bans and asset freezes on eighty-two Iranian officials for their involvement in human rights violations.[28] The new administration should consider additional designations to draw attention to Iran's poor human rights record and shore up EU support to maintain human- rights-related sanctions. (The EU must extend the restrictions annually.)

The Islamic Revolutionary Guards Corps

The IRGC controls a large portion of the country's economy,[29] and a number of its affiliates remain subject to U.S. and EU sanctions. As such, the application of U.S. secondary sanctions for dealings with IRGC affiliates remains a significant risk for companies looking to reengage with Iran. The engineering company Khatam al-Anbia (KACH) and a number of its subsidiaries, such as Sepanir Oil and Gas, which serves as the general contractor for part of the South Pars gas field, also remain on the UN sanctions list based on KACH's involvement in the construction of uranium enrichment sites at the Fordow enrichment plant.[30]

The United States, however, has yet to impose secondary sanctions for dealings with the IRGC. Testifying at a hearing before the House Committee on Foreign Affairs on February 11, 2016, John Smith, the acting director of OFAC, said that he was not aware of any violations of U.S. sanctions targeting the IRGC since JCPOA implementation.[31] To be sure, the legal threshold for applying secondary sanctions is actually quite high: while an IRGC affiliate need not be listed by OFAC to create exposure for banks (it only needs to have more than 50 percent IRGC ownership), the banks must have "knowingly" engaged in a "significant transaction" to qualify for sanctions. The IRGC can exploit this standard by establishing front companies and hiding ownership or subsidiaries through nontransparent structures, making it nearly impossible for foreign companies to identify the true beneficial ownership of their counterparty.

When it comes to strengthening implementation of sanctions against the IRGC, the United States could take several steps. First, the Treasury Department can and should designate additional IRGC subsidiaries and front companies, based on either IRGC ownership or control, under existing executive orders. Independent researchers have already identified dozens of unlisted IRGC affiliates based on publicly available information.[32] Second, either executive or congressional action could be taken to lower the ownership threshold. Such a move, however, would put a greater onus on banks to identify the IRGC affiliates blocked by "operation of law" but not included on published sanctions lists, which will remain a challenge as long as Iranian financial and commercial sectors lack greater transparency. Third, Congress has raised the specter of designating the IRGC a foreign terrorist organization (FTO). Legislation introduced by Sen. Ted Cruz (R-TX) in early January 2017 calls on the State Department to assess the IRGC's suitability for designation as an FTO.[33] While there is no doubt that elements of the IRGC, such as the Qods Force, have engaged in support for terrorism, a designation would do little to strengthen sanctions against the IRGC, since it has already been designated under other authorities. Moreover, such a move is unlikely to curry international support.

Strict Enforcement of SEC Reporting Requirements

While the JCPOA allows firms to conduct a variety of new types of business with Iran, the nuclear deal does not change the requirement that firms report to the U.S. government about their business with Iran. This fact needs to be brought vigorously to the attention of foreign firms, which must hear that failure to file the required reports will result in severe penalties. Disclosure of such ties, even if legally acceptable, could also trigger state-level divestment laws.

The reporting clause for business activities in Iran is located in Section 219 of the Securities and Exchange Commission (SEC) disclosure requirements, as mandated by the 2012 Iran Threat Reduction Act, with these requirements unaffected by the JCPOA.[34] Section 219 does not prohibit any conduct, but instead requires that issuers of publicly traded securities disclose in reports filed with the SEC any transaction with any part of the Iranian government, including the Central Bank; activities supporting the Iranian petroleum industry; facilitation of transactions with the IRGC; and transactions with persons sanctioned due to terrorism or weapons proliferations reasons.[35] Note that Section 219 applies not only to issuers of publicly traded securities but also to their "affiliates," which include joint ventures, foreign-registered subsidiaries, and controlling shareholders. Likewise, Section 219 contains no "materiality" threshold, meaning that it applies to all activities, no matter how small. Since Section 219 was imposed, firms from Brazil, China, India, Japan, Britain, Switzerland, and Turkey, among other countries, have filed more than a thousand reports.

Because Section 219 disclosure requirements remain in effect, any firm with publicly traded securities in the United States will face increased reporting requirements if that firm does business with Iran. For instance, European firms previously forbidden from buying Iranian crude oil may decide to restart such purchases; if so, Section 219 disclosure requirements will be triggered. At first, the SEC Office of Global Security Risk rigorously enforced Section 219, querying companies about disclosures that omitted information about potential activities with Iran suggested by press reports. The SEC should resume such rigorous enforcement.

CONSIDER NEW NONNUCLEAR SANCTIONS

In addition to more rigorously enforcing existing sanctions, the Trump administration should impose additional nonnuclear sanctions, especially for new transgressions by Iran. Even though the United States never pledged to refrain from applying nonnuclear sanctions for Iran's ongoing activities, linking new sanctions to Iran's post-JCPOA behavior may make it easier for Washington to gain international understanding that these new sanctions are nonnuclear rather than a rebranding of the older nuclear sanctions.

Cyber Sanctions

Cyber is emerging as a key tool in Iran's arsenal for dealing with both domestic and foreign threats.[36] Beyond the use of cyber tools for repression and monitoring of domestic opposition, a number of foreign attacks have been attributed to Iran in recent years. In August 2012, malware connected to Iran by U.S. intelligence officials destroyed data and disabled tens of thousands of Saudi Aramco computers.[37] The following month, hackers with ties to the Iranian government conducted a series of denial-of-service attacks primarily targeting the U.S. financial system, according to a March 2016 indictment of seven of the hackers.[38] List-based blocking sanctions put in place by authorities under Executive Order 13694 of April 1, 2015, allow for targeting of "significant malicious cyber-enabled activities." The authority, which was recently amended and deployed against Russian targets involved in cyber interference in the U.S. election, focused on the specific harms caused by significant malicious cyber-enabled activities, including threats to national security and critical infrastructure. Application of these sanctions could be used to expose Iranian entities involved in cyberattacks and create a possible deterrent to certain quasi-governmental and commercial actors within Iran, as well as foreign partners, from assisting in further development of Iranian offensive cyber capabilities.

Money Laundering

Another possible tool is the "311" finding of Iran as a jurisdiction of primary money-laundering concern. The 311 (which refers to Section 311 of the USA PATRIOT Act) authorizes the treasury secretary to pursue a range of measures against a financial institution, jurisdiction, or class of transaction found to be of "primary money-laundering concern." Associated with the finding against Iran in 2011, the Treasury Department issued a "notice of proposed rulemaking" calling for imposition of the "fifth special measure," which would require U.S. financial institutions to implement additional due diligence to prevent improper indirect access to the U.S. financial system by Iran or Iranian entities. The finding was based on "Iran's support for terrorism; pursuit of weapons of mass destruction (WMD); reliance on state-owned or controlled agencies to facilitate WMD proliferation; and the illicit and deceptive financial activities that Iranian financial institutions—including the Central Bank of Iran—and other state-controlled entities engage in to facilitate Iran's illicit conduct and evade sanctions."[39] There is little reason to believe that Iran's illicit financial conduct has ceased under the JCPOA. However, such regulatory measures are only implemented once a final rule has been issued, which was not done for the 311 on Iran. One option would be to make clear that this is a real option should FATF, the international standard-setting body for AML/CFT, remove Iran from its blacklist in June 2017 without Iran fulfilling the mutually agreed-on reforms under its FATF action plan.

Commerce Authorities

Somewhere between more rigorous implementation of existing restrictions and adoption of new sanctions would be fuller use of export controls. In part, this would mean devoting more resources and high-level attention to enforcing existing export controls. Generally speaking, this area gets woefully little attention and money because of the faulty perception that strict enforcement will cost U.S. jobs, when in fact most U.S. firms avoid questionable transactions. Thus, tighter enforcement will primarily affect foreign firms that incorporate U.S. products or technology in what they sell. In addition, it may well be appropriate to tighten export controls on products bound for Iran, such as products Iran is using for its cyberwarfare activities. Just by playing up export controls and their application to goods with more than 10 percent U.S.-origin content, the U.S. government could have a considerable chilling effect on those considering selling dual-use items to Iran. In sum, compliance with export controls is so complicated and resource-intensive that it is an underappreciated deterrent to commercial actors.

APPLY PROPORTIONAL SANCTIONS FOR JCPOA NONCOMPLIANCE

When Congress was considering the nuclear deal, the Obama administration insisted that it had reserved the right to apply proportional sanctions in the event of Iranian noncompliance with parts of the deal—that is, snapback of sanctions would not be an all-or-nothing proposition, nor would it depend on reaching consensus with the other major powers on whether Iran was complying with the deal's provisions. Adam Szubin, acting undersecretary of the treasury for terrorism and financial intelligence, acknowledged the concerns of international partners regarding minor violations by Iran when he noted in December 2015 that "we retain full flexibility, from partial measures to total snap back..."[40] That flexibility, the Obama team insisted, showed that the threat of snapback sanctions was real, rather than a purely theoretical provision.

Unfortunately, Iran may well not be complying with a part of the deal—not violating the deal so openly that the other major powers will agree that a full sanctions snapback is required but nevertheless calling for a firm U.S. response. In particular, Iran has made limited use of the nuclear procurement mechanism, set up by the JCPOA, through which Iran is supposed to acquire all foreign materials for its enrichment program. As of mid-January 2017, the mechanism had received only five requests to provide restricted goods to Iran, three of which had been approved and two that remained pending with the UN Security Council.[41] It is implausible that a nuclear program the size and scope of Iran's would need little from abroad. Indeed, the German government reported in summer 2016 that Iran continued to procure material for its nuclear program through other channels.[42] Washington should therefore insist on a discussion in the Joint Commission about Iran's obligations regarding this procurement mechanism. In its current approach, Iran claims no obligation to follow this mechanism, asserting the obligation belongs entirely to the government of the country where the supplier is located (this was also the Obama administration's interpretation). The Trump administration should devote intelligence community resources to identifying Iranian procurement occurring outside this mechanism.

Should clear evidence emerge indicating Iran is avoiding its obligations to use the procurement channel, Washington has the right under the agreement to trigger the mechanisms for full reimposition of nuclear sanctions. However, such a move would be an extreme reaction to a limited violation, and other countries quite possibly might not go along—helping explain why the nuclear deal's critics said the snapback provisions were unlikely to be invoked. Altogether, the United States should make clear that it reserves the right to impose appropriate sanctions even in the absence of international agreement on how to respond. Washington here needs to show that it does indeed reserve the right to act unilaterally against limited Iranian noncompliance: snapback is not all-or-nothing, nor is it contingent on complete agreement within the international community. The Obama administration claimed to be contemplating such unilateral and limited action in the case of limited Iranian noncompliance, so the Trump administration would be on firm ground adopting such a policy.

CONCLUSION

The new administration should develop, articulate, and implement a clear post-JCPOA sanctions policy based on the elements laid out in this paper: emphasizing the sanctions that remain; fully implementing those sanctions; and developing new nonnuclear sanctions and proportional responses to Iranian noncompliance with the JCPOA.

Allowing Iran to continue defining the success of the nuclear deal in terms of insufficient trade resumed or difficulty of financing obscures the role of Iran's nonnuclear behavior in dispelling potential commercial partners. Such behavior includes Iran's failure to abide by international norms both in moderating aggressive behavior in the region and in implementing reforms protecting its financial and commercial sectors from illicit financial activity and sanctions evasion. The Trump administration should therefore focus on Iran's conduct as the reason for the country's continuing isolation and the basis for a resumption of financial pressures.

While the administration has broad authority to shape sanctions policy and implementation, not all options are implementable, advisable, or should be employed immediately. First, there are limits to U.S. jurisdiction and the ability to compel foreign compliance. Consequently, policy should focus on building a broad coalition based on the consensus that Iranian behavior violates international norms. This is not to say that unilateral sanctions are useless. They can serve to communicate Iranian illicit activity and cause commercial actors to withdraw voluntarily from business based on reputational concerns, creating political openings for third countries to act. Second, Iran-specific changes to principles that underlie broader sanctions policy would complicate implementation. In such a case, direct action under existing authorities or the creation of new authorities is preferable to modifying guidance or enforcement. Finally, Congress is going to want to play a role in strengthening the role of sanctions in restraining Iran. The new administration and congress will need to work together to ensure that they are moving in the same direction.

KATHERINE BAUER, the Blumenstein-Katz Family Fellow at The Washington Institute, is a former Treasury official who served as the department's financial attaché in Jerusalem and the Gulf. She also served as the senior policy advisor for Iran and assistant director in the Office of Terrorist Financing and Financial Crimes.

NOTES

1. See http://washin.st/pnote38

2. "Treasury Sanctions Those Involved in Ballistic Missile Procurement for Iran," January 17, 2016, https://www.treasury.gov/press-center/press-releases/Pages/jl0322.aspx

3. "Iran Says Kerry's Remarks on Sanctions 'Unacceptable,'" *Gulf News*, October 17, 2016, http://gulfnews.com/news/mena/iran/iran-says-kerry-s-remarks-on-sanctions-unacceptable-1.1913911.

4. Kristina Wong, "U.S. General Sees 'Uptick' in Bad Behavior by Iran since Nuke Deal," *The Hill*, November 30, 2016, http://thehill.com/policy/defense/308151-us-general-sees-uptick-in-malign-iranian-activities-since-nuclear-deal#.WEBMCi_bCe4.twitter.

5. For more, see Katherine Bauer, "Iran Faces Challenges in Implementing Its FATF Action Plan," PolicyWatch 2717 (Washington Institute for Near East Policy, October 26, 2016), http://www.washingtoninstitute.org/policy-analysis/view/iran-faces-challenges-in-implementing-its-fatf-action-plan; see also Matthew Levitt and Katherine Bauer, "Iran's 'Resistance Economy'—and Stalled Reform Efforts," *Wall Street Journal*, September 23, 2016, http://blogs.wsj.com/washwire/2016/09/23/irans%E2%80%8B-resistance-economy-and-stalled-reform-efforts/?cb=logged0.8635195400458011.

6. Known formally as the Standard for Automatic Exchange of Financial Account Information, under the Convention on Mutual Administrative Assistance in Tax Matters. Some of the one hundred countries will begin the automatic exchange only in 2018.

7. JCPOA Annex II (about sanctions-lifting), Part B (what the U.S. government will do), Section 4.1.1., in which the deal expressly notes the U.S. pledge to cease applying sanctions on certain designated individuals and entities subject to sanctions under the Comprehensive Iran Sanctions, Accountability, and Divestment Act of 2010 (CISADA). The United States did not commit to lift CISADA. In fact, it is because CISADA still remains in effect that secondary sanctions apply to Iran-related individuals and entities designated under nonnuclear authorities.

8. JCPOA Annex II, Part B, footnote 12: "Should the United States determine that licensed aircraft, goods, or services have been used for purposes other than exclusively civil aviation end-use, or have been re-sold or re-transferred to persons on the SDN List, the United States would view this as grounds to cease performing its commitments under Section 5.1.1 in whole or in part." In other words, the consequence of using planes for anything other than "exclusively civil aviation end-use" is expressly written into the JCPOA.

9. Tom Odula, "Two Iranians Charged in Kenyan Court with Terrorism," Associated Press, December 1, 2016, http://bigstory.ap.org/article/baa8add6425841a9b54efb7f8bd56850/2-iranians-charged-kenyan-court-terrorism.

10. "The List Established and Maintained pursuant to Security Council Res. 2231 (2015)," United Nations, https://scsanctions.un.org/fop/fop?xml=htdocs/resources/xml/en/consolidated.xml&xslt=htdocs/resources/xsl/en/iran.xsl.

11. Emanuele Ottolenghi, "Flying in the Face of U.S. Sanctions," *Wall Street Journal*, February 3, 2016, http://www.wsj.com/articles/flying-in-the-face-of-u-s-sanctions-1454531168.

12. "First Iran Flight Lands in Shiite-Held Yemen Capital," *National*, March 1, 2015, http://www.thenational.ae/world/middle-east/first-iran-flight-lands-in-shiite-held-yemen-capital.

13. Mohammed Ali Kalfood and Kareem Fahim, "Saudis Hit a Yemeni Airport, Possibly Closing Aid Route," *New York Times*, April 28, 2015, http://www.nytimes.com/2015/04/29/world/middleeast/saudis-hit-a-yemeni-airport-possibly-closing-aid-route.html.

14. See Mahan Air Press Room, http://www.mahan.aero/en/contact/press-room.

15. See Mahan Air International Route Network, http://www.mahan.aero/en/destinations/route-network.

16. U.S. Department of the Treasury, "Treasury Designates Syrian Entity, Others Involved in Arms and Communications Procurement Networks and Identifies Blocked Iranian Aircraft," press release, September 19, 2012, https://www.treasury.gov/press-center/press-releases/Pages/tg1714.aspx.

17. U.S. Department of the Treasury, "Treasury Department Targets Those Involved in Iranian Scheme to Purchase Airplanes," press release, May 21, 2015, https://www.treasury.gov/press-center/press-releases/Pages/jl10061.aspx.

18. U.S. Department of the Treasury, "Treasury Sanctions Supporters of Iran's Ballistic Missile Program and Terrorism-Designated Mahan Air," press release, March 24, 2016, https://www.treasury.gov/press-center/press-releases/Pages/jl0395.aspx.

19. Sami Aboudi, "Saudi Arabia Suspends Iran's Mahan Air License to Use Its Air Space," Reuters, April 4, 2016, http://www.reuters.com/article/us-saudi-iran-aviation-idUSKCN0X123L.

20. U.S. Department of the Treasury, "Testimony of Acting Under Secretary for Terrorism and Financial Intelligence Adam J. Szubin before the House Committee on Foreign Affairs," press release, May 25, 2016, https://www.treasury.gov/press-center/press-releases/Pages/jl0466.aspx.

21. U.S. Drug Enforcement Administration, "DEA and European Authorities Uncover Massive Hizballah Drug and Money Laundering Scheme," February 1, 2016, https://www.dea.gov/divisions/hq/2016/hq020116.shtml.

22. Peter Kenyon, "Did Iran's Ballistic Missile Test Violate A U.N. Resolution?" *NPR Parallels*, February 3, 2017, http://www.npr.org/sections/parallels/2017/02/03/513229839/did-irans-ballistic-missile-test-violate-a-u-n-resolution.

23. U.S. Department of State, "Executive Order 13382—Blocking Property of Weapons of Mass Destruction Proliferators and Their Supporters," July 1, 2005, http://www.state.gov/documents/organization/135435.pdf.

24. U.S. Department of the Treasury, "Treasury Sanctions Supporters of Iran's Ballistic Missile Program and Terrorism-Designated Mahan Air," press release, March 24, 2016, https://www.treasury.gov/press-center/press-releases/Pages/jl0395.aspx.

25. U.S. Department of the Treasury, "Treasury Targets Iranian Arms Shipments," press release, March 27, 2012, https://www.treasury.gov/press-center/press-releases/Pages/tg1506.aspx.

26. Ibid.

27. U.S. Department of the Treasury, "Treasury Sanctions Iranian Security Forces for Human Rights Abuses," press release, June 9, 2011, https://www.treasury.gov/press-center/press-releases/Pages/tg1204.aspx.

28. "Council Decision (CFSP) 2016/565 Amending Decision 2011/235/CFSP concerning Restrictive Measures Directed against Certain Persons and Entities in View of the Situation in Iran," *Official Journal of the European Union*, April 12, 2016, http://eur-lex.europa.eu/legal-content/EN/TXT/PDF/?uri=CELEX:32016D0565&qid=1460465337598&from=EN.

29. Greg Bruno, Jayshree Bajoria, and Jonathan Masters, "Iran's Revolutionary Guards," *CFR Backgrounder*, Council on Foreign Relations, June 14, 2013, http://www.cfr.org/iran/irans-revolutionary-guards/p14324.

30. United Nations, "Security Council Imposes Additional Sanctions on Iran, Voting 12 in Favour to 2 Against, with 1 Abstention," June 9, 2010, http://www.un.org/press/en/2010/sc9948.doc.htm.

31. "Iran Nuclear Deal Oversight: Implementation and Its Consequences," hearing before the Committee on Foreign Affairs, U.S. House of Representatives, February 11, 2016, http://docs.house.gov/meetings/FA/FA00/20160211/104456/HHRG-114-FA00-Transcript-20160211.pdf.

32. See Annex I of 2015 testimony by Emanuele Ottolenghi before the House Committee on Foreign Affairs for a list of publicly traded companies in which the IRGC is a shareholder. The document contains active links to Tehran Stock Exchange ownership information. As Ottolenghi notes in his testimony, in a number of cases, ostensible ownership is held by undesignated IRGC affiliates whereas effective ownership and control by designated individuals or entities is obscured through the chain of fronts: "The Iran Nuclear Deal and Its Impact on Iran's Islamic Revolutionary Guard Corps," September 17, 2015, http://www.defenddemocracy.org/content/uploads/documents/Ottolenghi_HFAC_IranDeal_IRGC.pdf.

33. U.S. Senate Foreign Relations Committee, "S.67—A bill to direct the secretary of state to submit to Congress a report on the designation of Iran's Revolutionary Guard Corps as a Foreign Terrorist Organization, and for other purposes," 115th Congress (2017–18), https://www.congress.gov/bill/115th-congress/senate-bill/67/text?q=%7B%22search%22%3A%5B%22S.67%22%5D%7D&r=1.

34. This discussion of Section 219 draws heavily on Marik String and David Horn, "As Iran Sanctions Wane, SEC Reporting Will Not," *Securities Regulation & Law Report*, January 2016, available at https://www.wilmerhale.com/uploadedFiles/Shared_Content/Editorial/Publications/Documents/2016-01-26-Bloomberg-BNA-As-Iran-Sanctions-Wane-SEC-Reporting-Will-Not.pdf.

35. In a further complication for compliance, Section 219 exempts from disclosure dealings with the government of Iran if undertaken pursuant to a U.S. government license. It is not clear if that includes the general licenses issues by OFAC; see https://www.treasury.gov/resource-center/sanctions/Documents/hr_1905_pl_112_158.pdf, p. 22.

36. See Michael Eisenstadt, *Iran's Lengthening Cyber Shadow*, Research Note 34 (Washington DC: Washington Institute, 2016), http://www.washingtoninstitute.org/uploads/Documents/pubs/ResearchNote34_Eisenstadt.pdf.

37. Nicole Perlroth, "In Cyberattack on Saudi Firm, U.S. Sees Iran Firing Back," *New York Times*, October 23, 2016, http://www.nytimes.com/2012/10/24/business/global/cyberattack-on-saudi-oil-firm-disquiets-us.html.

38. Dustin Volz and Jim Finkle, "U.S. Indicts Iranians for Hacking Dozens of Banks, New York Dam," Reuters, March 25, 2016, http://www.reuters.com/article/us-usa-iran-cyber-idUSKCN0WQ1JF.

39. U.S. Department of the Treasury, "Fact Sheet: New Sanctions on Iran," press release, November 21, 2011, https://www.treasury.gov/press-center/press-releases/Pages/tg1367.aspx.

40. U.S. Department of the Treasury, "Remarks by Acting Under Secretary for Terrorism and Financial Intelligence Adam Szubin at the Atlantic Council and the Iran Project Symposium," press release, December 17, 2015, https://www.treasury.gov/press-center/press-releases/Pages/jl0304.aspx.

41. United Nations, Second report of the Secretary-General on the implementation of Security Council resolution 2231 (2015), 30 December 2016, http://www.un.org/ga/search/view_doc.asp?symbol=S/2016/1136.

42. Ryan Browne, "German Intelligence: Iran May Have Tried to Violate Nuclear Deal," CNN, July 8, 2016, http://www.cnn.com/2016/07/08/politics/germany-iran-violate-nuclear-deal/.

"Iran on Notice: The Future of U. S. Policy on Iran"

David Albright
President, Institute for Science and International Security

Testimony of David Albright,
President of the
Institute for Science and International Security,
before the House Foreign Affairs Committee

Hearing Title: "Iran on Notice"

February 16, 2017

The Joint Comprehensive Plan of Action (JCPOA) needs to be implemented more effectively, its nuclear conditions strengthened, and its verification improved. Its implementation has been too permissive and tolerant of Iran's behavior to violate the deal, exploit loopholes, avoid critical verification requirements, and generally push the envelope of allowed behavior. Too often concessions have been made from a misplaced fear that Iran would walk away from the deal or somehow President Rouhani's presidency needed protecting. However, the deal can be better enforced by the United States without leading to its termination. As a matter of policy, the Trump administration should close key loopholes in the agreement and move to correct its short- and long-term deficiencies.

At its heart, the Iran deal is a bet that by the time the nuclear limitations end, Iran, the region, or both will have changed so much that Iran will no longer seek nuclear weapons. But despite immense sanctions relief, Iran has been increasing its conventional military power and regional hegemony, and threatening its neighbors. The bet does not appear to be winnable under the current circumstances.

Those who argued that the nuclear deal would moderate Iran's behavior in the region have sadly been disappointed. Moreover, a trade of prisoners for hostages only encouraged Iran to seize more Americans. Armed with substantial funds and a growing economy, Iran is challenging the United States in the region and appears as committed to maintaining the capability to pursue a nuclear weapons path as before, just a longer path.

When the major nuclear limitations end, Iran has stated it will have an industrial-size enrichment program, poised to break out within days or weeks. It will have developed advanced centrifuges that would enable a quick sneak out to nuclear weapons. It is mastering long-range, nuclear-capable ballistic missiles including possibly intercontinental nuclear-tipped ballistic missiles. This Iranian nuclear future is unacceptable. A solution needs to thought through and a remediation path developed.

Dealing with the short-term implementation mistakes and fixing JCPOA loopholes and deficiencies need to be priorities. Although the nuclear deal should not be abrogated, as it has many benefits, the deal must be implemented differently and strengthened.

Taking Stock of Implementation

Iran continues to test ballistic missiles that are inconsistent with, or to some in the administration, in violation of UN Security Council resolution 2231. Iran's ongoing development of missiles capable of carrying nuclear weapons is a direct threat to the nuclear deal. A nuclear weapon should be properly defined as a nuclear warhead and a delivery system. This definition was used by South Africa for its nuclear weapons program back in the 1980s, when that program was active and engaged in intense secrecy and obfuscation to deceive the world. It too denied that its missiles would ever carry nuclear weapons, a fact it admitted only after it verifiably abandoned its nuclear weapons program in the early 1990s. As the administration and Congress chart a new Iran nuclear policy, Iran's ballistic missile program should be viewed as the other half of a nuclear weapon whose development continues unabated today and should be treated accordingly.

What are some of the specific problems in the nuclear deal's implementation? First, the workings of the deal have been far too secret. Some portions of the parallel or side deals and secret Joint Commission and Procurement Working Group (PWG) decisions and actions have been publicly revealed. Although the Joint Commission decided after Donald Trump won the presidency to release its major decisions, likely feeling increasing pressure to do so, much still remains secret. Moreover, the International Atomic Energy Agency (IAEA) continues to underreport the actual situation on the ground.

Many of the Joint Commission decisions are questionable. Too much low enriched uranium (LEU) was exempted from the JCPOA 300 kilogram LEU cap, and too many hot cells in violation of the deal's size limits were allowed to continue to operate. Iran was allowed to exceed its cap of 130 metric tons of heavy water by over 70 metric tons via a loophole in the JCPOA to secretly cache heavy water in Oman while awaiting its sale.[1] A sounder interpretation of the deal, and one more in U.S. interests, would have been to apply the 130 metric ton cap to all the heavy water under Iran's control or ownership regardless of location, thereby requiring Iran to blend at least 70 metric tons of heavy water down to normal water and not ship it out to Oman in the first place.

So far, Iran has resisted IAEA inspections of military sites. Although Iran has granted access to nuclear sites, it has reportedly resisted granting access to military locations associated with past undeclared nuclear activities or potentially involved in nuclear weapons development activities banned under the JCPOA. To this day, the IAEA has not been able to state that Iran has addressed its concerns and questions about past nuclear weapons activities or to determine the exact status of what Iran achieved and may have hidden away. In addition to past activities, the IAEA has not stated that it is successfully verifying the JCPOA's prohibitions on specific nuclear weapons development activities, which would require access to military sites.

---

[1] See for example, *Heavy Water Loophole in the Iran Deal*, by David Albright and Andrea Stricker, Institute for Science and International Security Report, December 21, 2016. http://isis-online.org/isis-reports/detail/heavy-water-loophole-in-the-iran-deal

The poorly designed arrangement between Iran and the IAEA on Parchin not surprisingly failed to resolve the issue. It also put the IAEA in a weak position to move forward on accessing the Parchin site to resolve this issue, which includes making sense out of uranium particles detected by environmental sampling at Parchin. The presence of these particles combined with all the previous, suspicious site alterations is dramatic evidence that Iran conducted secret nuclear weapons activities at Parchin, despite its on-going denials.

Iran's refusal to let the IAEA resolve Parchin issues or regularly visit military sites is a major blemish on the JCPOA. It undermines any argument that the Iran deal is adequately verified.

Moreover, out of a misplaced fear of negatively affecting the deal, the Obama administration also interfered in U.S. law enforcement efforts. During the negotiations and for some time afterwards, the administration blocked or did not process several extradition requests and lure memos aimed at arresting and convicting Iranians and their agents engaged in breaking U.S. export and sanctions laws. These actions, largely concentrated in the State Department, reportedly interfered with investigations and served to discourage new or on-going federal investigations of commodity trafficking involving Iran.

The Procurement Working Group recently allowed Iran to acquire 149 metric tons of natural uranium. Iran's nuclear chief said last week that Iran would have 60 percent more stockpiled uranium than it did prior to the deal. Ali Akbar Salehi, the head of the Atomic Energy Organization of Iran, was quoted by the semi-official Fars News Agency stating that Iran would receive a final batch of 149 tons of natural uranium, in addition to 210 tons already delivered since early 2016. The 149 metric tons was a swap for sending part of its cache of heavy water in Oman to Russia, heavy water that should have been blended down into normal water instead, if the deal had been seriously enforced. Interestingly, the caching of heavy water in Oman and the decision to approve sending natural uranium to Iran were considered secret by the Joint Commission and the Obama administration. These 149 metric tons, if enriched to weapon-grade uranium, would be enough for over 15 nuclear weapons.

The Atomic Energy Organization of Iran has sought sensitive nuclear-related materials and facilities, in at least two cases knowing that the supplier country would deny the exports. Under the deal, Iran can ask for whatever it wants overseas and does not have to report it. The supplier is the one that must seek the permission from its government and the Procurement Working Group. This loophole lays the basis for secret Iranian illicit procurement efforts with less scrupulous suppliers and countries.

Mechanisms for Obtaining Improvements

There are several mechanisms to better enforce and strengthen the Iran deal both in the short and long term. The United States can take unilateral steps within the context of the JCPOA, such as by blocking proposals for goods going to Iran via the Procurement Working Group or blocking further exemptions to the 300 kilogram cap. The United States can press for strengthening measures in the Joint Commission, the executive body of the JCPOA. In fact, under U.S. leadership, the Joint Commission did strengthen the condition in the JCPOA on near 20 percent enriched uranium. The Joint Commission added a new condition that any fuel containing near

20 percent LEU would have to be irradiated; none could be stored as fresh or unirradiated fuel. Although this step of irradiating the fuel will not affect breakout timelines that significantly, it is a precedent for the ability of the Joint Commission to add conditions to the deal.

The United States can encourage the IAEA to better verify conditions in the JCPOA. There are many possibilities, including the IAEA more thoroughly monitoring the use of several large hot cells in Iran exempted for use outside JCPOA size limitations and the inspectors cracking down on Iran's attempts to push the envelope on centrifuge R&D activities. The United States can press the IAEA to use its rights to access military sites or personnel in Iran in furtherance of effective JCPOA verification. In addition, parallel agreements between Iran and the IAEA can be negotiated that enshrine the IAEA's access to Parchin or other military sites or create work plans to settle outstanding verification issues associated with reaching a broader conclusion under the Additional Protocol.

A final option is to negotiate a JCPOA II and a new UN Security Council resolution. These efforts, which would take a while to launch, could focus on repairing major weaknesses in the deal associated with the duration of the nuclear limitations and ballistic missiles.

Short Term Priorities for the Administration

The administration should announce that the United States will demonstrate zero tolerance for Iranian violations of the JCPOA, no matter how small, and will respond both within and outside the context of the JCPOA. Where violations are significant or the frequency of minor infractions reach a threshold, the United States should snap back UN sanctions.

The administration should state that it now views the following as not allowed by, and even in some cases inconsistent with, the JCPOA: (1) heavy water excess being cached overseas, e.g. in Oman, awaiting sale, (2) Iran selling any heavy water without a proposal submitted to the PWG, (3) exemptions of low enriched uranium from the 300 kilogram cap, except in extraordinary circumstances (such as for a modified Arak reactor) (4) lack of regular IAEA access to Iranian military sites, (5) enrichment of depleted uranium to natural uranium outside the 300 kilogram cap, (6) Iran not reporting to the Joint Commission about any request for nuclear or nuclear-related goods, and (7) Iranian cooperation with North Korea.

Specific Steps to Ensure Stricter Enforcement and Strengthening of the JCPOA in the Short Term

- **Achieving Greater Transparency and IAEA Access**
  - Pressing the IAEA to include greater details in its quarterly reports to the Board of Governors.[2]

---

[2] The quarterly reports should include Iran's total inventory of enriched uranium stocks and their chemical forms and how much is included in the 300 kg cap and how much exempted from this cap; Iran's quarterly enrichment production output at Natanz; status of stable isotope production efforts at Fordow and elsewhere; natural uranium production and imports; heavy water quarterly production and total inventory domestically and in Oman or other off-shore locations; status and progress in centrifuge R&D and reporting on the number of manufactured centrifuges rotor assemblies; status of construction and operation of advanced centrifuge assembly facilities at Natanz;

- o Pressing the IAEA to provide details about its plans and progress in reaching a broader conclusion and ensuring the absence of undeclared nuclear materials and activities in Iran.
- o Publicly releasing parallel agreements to the JCPOA, including Iran's long term enrichment R&D plan and the agreement regarding Iran's ability to limit inspections at Parchin.
- o Ensuring that Iran provides guaranteed, timely IAEA access to Iranian military facilities, consistent with the access timeframes in the Additional Protocol, where the IAEA suspects nuclear-related activities have occurred or it needs access to verify specified JCPOA bans on nuclear weapons development activities.

- **Preventing Iran Developing an Indigenous Enriched Uranium Fuel Fabrication Capability**
  - o Ensuring and taking steps at the Joint Commission and Procurement Working Group so that Iran does not research, develop, or import a domestic enriched uranium fuel manufacturing capability. Toward that goal, further exemptions to the 300 kilogram enriched uranium cap should be deferred indefinitely.
  - o Reviewing all civil reactor sales to Iran with the goal of ensuring that these sales include a minimum of a ten-year fuel supply that is renewable for the life of the reactor and do not include the transfer of fuel fabrication or hot cell facilities in whole or in part. The goal should be to ensure a lifetime of fuel for any reactor provided to Iran and the absence of the supply of fuel fabrication capabilities and hot cells associated with fuel development or testing.

- **Plugging Loopholes in the JCPOA**
  - o Closing the Oman loophole for heavy water. To that end, all shipments of Iranian heavy water from Oman (or other overseas storage locations) would be subject to approval by the Procurement Working Group.
  - o Banning research and development of naval reactors, including land prototypes.
  - o Closing the loophole whereby Iran enriches depleted uranium to natural uranium, unless the product (albeit natural uranium) is considered part of the 300 kilogram LEU cap.
  - o Investigating, reviewing, strictly interpreting, and ensuring Iran is abiding by restrictions on centrifuge R&D under the JCPOA. One example is allegations that Iran is exploiting allowed "quality assurance" criteria at Kalaye Electric and possibly elsewhere to conduct additional mechanical testing of centrifuges beyond that allowed under the JCPOA.

---

locations, characterizations, and monitoring of hot cells; work carried out to date on the Arak reactor; as well as other nuclear activities. The report should also discuss controversies with Iran over interpretation or implementation of JCPOA conditions and the comprehensive safeguards agreement and associated Additional Protocol, as well as progress or problems in reaching a broader conclusion.

o Reviewing the existing conditions on near 20 percent low enriched uranium to determine their adequacy, including evaluating the raising of the radiation limit imposed on fresh LEU fuel from its current relatively low level.

- **Strengthening the Procurement Working Group**
  o Reviewing the operation of the Procurement Working Group, including lengthening by several weeks the period for the review of submitted proposals.
  o Requiring that Iran report any requests for nuclear or nuclear-related goods to the Joint Commission and Procurement Working Group.

- **Creating an Iranian Export Control System**
  o Insisting that Iran create and implement a strategic trade control system that meets international standards and that will be subject to review by the Joint Commission. According to the JCPOA, "Iran *intends* to apply nuclear export policies and practices in line with the internationally established standards for the export of nuclear material, equipment and technology (emphasis added)."[3] Iran has not committed to do so, and Tehran could interpret this condition far differently than the United States. As part of creating a strategic trade control regime in Iran, the United States should also interpret the JCPOA as stating that Iran will commit not to conduct illicit commodity trafficking for government controlled or owned military, missile, nuclear, or other industries and programs, and it will agree to enforce this ban on private Iranian companies. Conducting illicit commodity trafficking is not in line with internationally established standards for strategic trade control systems.

- **Creating More Effective Enforcement of Trading Bans and Sanctions**
  o Stepping up efforts with allies to detect, interdict, or otherwise thwart Iran's illicit procurement efforts that violate national and international laws.
  o The Department of Justice committing to more aggressively investigating, indicting, and extraditing those involved in outfitting Iran's nuclear, missile, or conventional weapons programs in defiance of U.S. laws and sanctions. As discussed above, during the last administration, there was excessive denial or non-processing of extradition requests and lure memos out of a misplaced concern about their effect on the Iran nuclear deal. These actions, largely concentrated in the State Department, reportedly interfered with investigations and served to discourage new or on-going federal investigations of commodity trafficking involving Iran. This trend needs to be reversed by an administration-wide policy to encourage investigations of Iranian (and other pariah state) commodity trafficking efforts that includes a determined extradition process.

---

[3] JCPOA, Annex 1, par. 73: "Iran intends to apply nuclear export policies and practices in line with the internationally established standards for the export of nuclear material, equipment and technology. For 15 years, Iran will only engage, including through export of any enrichment or enrichment related equipment and technology, with any other country, or with any foreign entity in enrichment or enrichment related activities, including related research and development activities, following approval by the Joint Commission."

- o Reviewing past U.S. lure and extradition requests relating to Iran as to the feasibility and practicality of the State Department belatedly approving them.
- o Taking steps to better detect and block Iranian cooperation with North Korea on ballistic missiles, cruise missiles, and conventional arms. Devoting more intelligence resources to determining if North Korea and Iran are cooperating on nuclear programs or transferring nuclear technology, equipment, or materials.

Longer Term Improvements

The Iran deal has fundamental long-term deficiencies that need to be addressed. Which problems to focus on and how to remedy them should be part of an Iran policy review by the Trump administration. A few recommended remedies are ensuring:

- Limits on the enrichment level and a 12 month breakout requirement remain in place in perpetuity. This would involve addressing the JCPOA's phased lifting of restrictions on Iran's enrichment capabilities at year 10 and after.
- Full resolution of the outstanding issues about Iran's past secret nuclear activities, including those associated with the "possible military dimensions" of Iran's nuclear programs.
- An effective verification regime able to ensure an absence of undeclared nuclear material and facilities in Iran and adequate warning of major violations.
- Limits on Iranian ballistic missile development, testing, and production.

Conclusion

The Trump administration appears committed to maintaining the JCPOA. This decision makes good sense. But the administration also recognizes that if the deal is to survive and serve U.S. national security interests, the JCPOA needs to be more strictly enforced and interpreted, and its most significant weaknesses need to be corrected.

"Iran on Notice: The Future of U. S. Policy on Iran"

Andrew Exum
Former Deputy Assistant Secretary of Defense for Middle East Policy

DR. ANDREW EXUM

TESTIMONY BEFORE THE FOREIGN AFFAIRS COMMITTEE

Mr. Chairman, Mr. Ranking Member, thank you so much for the opportunity to speak to the committee today.

I've been asked to present testimony on Iran, and I'll do so in my capacity as the former deputy assistant secretary of defense for Middle East policy in the Obama Administration. I left the Department of Defense last month, and my testimony today was cleared by the Department to ensure what I tell you remains at the appropriate level of classification. I don't need to remind any of you, though, that restricting our discussion to the unclassified level constrains what I can say about the way in which the Obama Administration addressed the challenges posed by Iran.

The United States has three vital interests in the Middle East: the security of the state of Israel, countering terrorism and the proliferation of weapons of mass destruction, and freedom of navigation and commerce in and around the Arabian Peninsula, which as you all know is home to vast hydrocarbon reserves.

Iran can and does pose a threat to all of those interests, and it does so in three ways: its nuclear program, its build-up of conventional arms, and what we call its asymmetric activities – its support to proxies such as Hizballah or some of the Shia militias in Iraq.

During the Obama Administration, we countered Iran through what we called our four Ps: our posture, our plans, our partners, and our preparedness.

With respect to our posture, we have about 35,000 troops in and around the Persian Gulf alone. We have major air bases in Kuwait, Qatar, and the United Arab Emirates. We have a major naval base in Bahrain. These bases and the troops operating out of them allow us to both ensure freedom of navigation in and around the Arabian Peninsula, combat terror groups – for many of these troops are currently busy in the skies over Iraq and Syria – and deter conventional Iranian aggression against our Gulf partners.

We maintain a robust suite of plans to respond to regional contingencies. In my capacity at the Department of Defense, I reviewed these plans. They are real, they are resourced, and our forces are ready to execute them.

Over the past three decades, meanwhile, we have invested in our regional partnerships, and specifically, building capacity in our Gulf partners. We have a long way to go, but one of the areas where we have made the most progress – ballistic missile defense – helps us counter Iran's build-up of conventional weapons. We also engaged in unprecedented levels of defense and intelligence cooperation with Israel while making available some of our most advanced U.S.-made weapons to Gulf partners.

Finally, we have our preparedness. We chose this word because we needed a fourth "p," frankly, but what this really stands for is the many dozens of unilateral, bilateral, and multilateral exercises we conduct on an annual basis to help us prepare for regional contingencies.

So how are we doing? I'll be blunt in my assessment and then offer some words of advice for this new administration as well as some words of caution for this committee. Specifically, I will argue that this administration's strategic flirtation with Russia is incompatible with what I assess to be its desire to pressure and counter Iran.

First, the Department of Defense did not play a role in negotiating the nuclear deal with Iran, but the deal very much helps the U.S. military. Despite all the *sturm und drang* here in Washington and elsewhere in the summer of 2015, most strategic planners with whom I have spoken – both here and in the region – see the deal as offering real, positive opportunities to both the United States and Iran.

As you know, the Department of Defense was always in charge of providing the enforcement mechanism for U.S. policy. If Iran cheats, we will know about it, and the Department of Defense is prepared to act accordingly. From our perspective, then, the nuclear deal was a pretty good deal because it constrained Iran while placing no such constraints on us.

Iran also has some opportunities, of course, and it appears to be largely squandering them. Some optimists in the Obama Administration had hoped the nuclear negotiations would be a way to bring Iran in from the cold, so to speak, and encourage Iran to play a more helpful role regionally. The view of these optimists was not universally shared within the administration: many of us argued within the administration and to our allies that the reason we needed to sign this deal with Iran was not because Iran is a benign actor but because it is a malign actor – and thus needed to be prevented from acquiring nuclear weapons. Iran's actions since signing the nuclear deal have somewhat vindicated us pessimists.

Iran continues a robust build-up of conventional weapons – including what we military folks would call anti-access, area denial weapons like anti-ship cruise missiles and air defense systems. I don't think our military commanders are losing sleep over these weapons systems just yet, but I know our regional partners are. Here's my first word of caution: these weapons systems, for the most part, are not indigenous to the Islamic Republic of Iran. These are Russian weapons, sold by Russia to Iran, with the aim of constraining U.S. freedom of maneuver in strategically important waterways and airways. Any serious effort to counter the build-up of these Iranian capabilities, then, has to take Russia into account.

Iran is also continuing what I will call its asymmetric activities. Its support to Shia and allied militia in Lebanon, Iraq, Syria, and Yemen continues. The presence of anti-ship cruise missiles into Yemen is especially concerning since it threatens a key commercial waterway, the Bab al-Mandeb.

Let me be blunt again regarding the administration's overtures to Russia: in Syria, it will be exceptionally difficult and likely impossible to reach any kind of accommodation with Russia and the regime in Damascus that does not end up strengthening Iran and its proxies, including Hizballah. So before the administration goes down that path, they should recognize that in the short term at least, they are going to embolden some of the very people they have pledged to counter in the region. And they will embolden Iran and these groups to the detriment of Israel's security.

In Iraq, meanwhile, the Islamic State is on a clear path to defeat. But the long-term threat to Iraq's sovereignty is both Kurdish separatism and the Shia militias – many of them supported by Iran – that exist only loosely affiliated with the Iraqi state. In addition, Iraq's long-term stability will be dependent on the United States being able to keep a small contingent of trainers and special operators in the country – which is why the president's dismissive comments about the Iraqi government, his comments about how we should have taken Iraq's oil, and his ban on Iraqis coming to the United

States have been so strategically misguided. This all plays into the narrative of an Iran that very much views Iraq as a zero-sum game with the United States and has spent millions of dollars to convince Iraqis that we have the kind of malign attitudes toward Iraq that the president seems to, in fact, actually have but which few others share. If the United States wants to push back on that, it needs to do so in the president's words and with robust diplomacy. I would caution the administration from trying to push back on Iran or its proxies militarily in Iraq – at least for now. We still have a Sunni terrorist enemy to defeat in Iraq, and our 5,000 troops in Iraq need to focus on the fight against the Islamic State, not war with Iran's proxies. I fought in Iraq, and any of us who served there remember the ways in which Iran can make life miserable for U.S. troops there. We don't need that fight right now.

Finally, a few words on Yemen. We've talked about Islamic fundamentalism, but I'm somewhat of a freedom of navigation fundamentalist: the United States should be prepared to robustly counter any threats to key waterways, and I'm not going to lose any sleep if a couple of Houthis die because they made the error of firing an anti-ship cruise missile into the Bab al-Mandeb. I should note, though, that the vast, vast majority of commercial traffic – roughly 1,400 vessels, or 80 million tons – that flows

through the Bab al-Mandeb on a monthly basis is not American: it is from

the European Union, India, China, and Korea. Those are the countries that

have the most at stake in any actions which threaten shipping through the

Bab al-Mandeb, and before the administration escalates a war in Yemen, it

should start with some multilateral diplomacy telling Iran, in essence, to

knock it off lest its own commercial interests fall under threat.

In Secretary Mattis, we have a Secretary of Defense who keenly understands

the threat posed by Iran. And in Secretary Tillerson and Gary Cohn, we

have, respectively, a Secretary of State and a Director of the Economic

Council who understand the centrality of market access to hydrocarbon

resources in the Gulf to the global economy.

So there's some cause for optimism that this administration will eventually

put together a coherent strategy to counter Iran's malign activities in a way

that serves U.S. interests. But the contradictions in the administration's

strategic initiatives thus far, not to mention the alarming dysfunction within

the national security decision-making process, leave plenty of room for

worry as well.

www.ingramcontent.com/pod-product-compliance
Lightning Source LLC
Chambersburg PA
CBHW081424280526
45788CB00009B/3220